The Calm Throughout Life's Storms

God-given Heartfelt Poetry

by

Tamra Cantore

INKWATER
PRESS

Dedication

This book is dedicated with love to my children Christina and Ben and my husband Jim. Thank you for allowing me the honor of sharing this God-given gift. I pray that in their own small way donations from the sale of this book will help in finding a cure, so that someday you will see your Mommy (and wife) without her shaking and see her walk without stumbling. This is not the life which we would have chosen for ourselves, but how awesome God is to be able to use a broken vessel like me for the glory of His Kingdom. God made each of us exactly as He wanted, to fulfill His purpose for our lives. Remember, you were wonderfully made and you are perfect in God's eyes through your love of Jesus.

I also want to extend my Love and appreciation for on-going understanding and support from:

- My Dad ("CEO" of my fan club) and his extended family. The greatest gift you ever gave me was telling me that my poetry brought you closer to the Lord! Thank you for being my biggest cheerleader.
- My Mom and the Hussey extended family. Mom, thanks for your model of caring and sensitivity which I cherish. And to the Hussey Men and families, thank you for making Mom, Shel and me feel like a real part of your family and for caring for Grandpa before he passed away.
- My sister Shelee - the one who understands and knows me best (and likes me anyway). And to her three wonderful Christian children and their extended families. Thanks for being such a big part of my family's life and being understanding and compassionate to us throughout all of our challenges. I can't tell you what joy it brings me when you call for advice or want to come visit us. I couldn't ask for more than that!
- My in-laws and the Cantore extended family. Thank you for accepting me into your family and treating me like one of your own. Your support and encouragement is so very much appreciated.
- Ms. Wanda and her son Rob - God was truly looking after us when he sent us His angel, Wanda. No one could love our kids more than Ms. Wanda (all of us "kids"). The unconditional love and her gift of service are priceless. And, when we brought

Wanda into our family, we got a bonus blessing...her son Rob. He always expects the best he can get out of the kids and has helped them achieve milestones even my husband and I thought were unachievable.

I pray that the legacy I leave for each of you is a love for the Lord so that you may experience the same joy and peace I have found as I put my trust in my Savior Jesus Christ.

In Memory of:

Tamra's Grandfather, Richard M. Zinn
Tamra's Grandfather, Ferris Hitchcock
Tamra's co-worker and friend Deborah Arildsen

In Honor of:

Tamra's "adopted" God-Father, Glenn Burgeson
Special TEAM CANTORE members:
Patricia Sanborn and Orville Scott
Tamra's PD Pals: Kimerly Coshow & Patty Labounty

More Praise for
The Calm Throughout Life's Storms

"It's been my privilege to share in the ministry works of Tamra Cantore. Her heartfelt and beautiful expressions of poetry are clearly reflective of an authentic walk with Jesus Christ in her life. It is a blessing to observe how Tamra allows God to use whatever circumstances come her way to bring honor to the Lord through the eloquence and depth of her writings. The words and meaning within the words that God places in Tamra inspire and encourage every reader."

> - **Mark Cottingham**; *Associate Pastor, Worship and Music, Johnson Ferry Baptist Church; Marietta, Ga.*

"God can use all our trials (including physical) for His honor and glory. In our family...my wife has had 30 years of major challenges with rheumatoid arthritis...my older daughter, 23 years of major challenges with juvenile diabetes. As a result of 9/11 my business was dramatically affected resulting in financial stress. Because of our experience with trials and seeing how God comforts us so we can comfort others (II Corinthians 1:3-4)...when we met Tamra and read her poetry we quickly saw how God was using her challenges to His honor and glory. Tamra has been such an encouragement to many, many people already...as her poetry is seen by more and more people, I am sure her reputation as a comforter of multitudes will be a reality."

> - **Ted Sprague, Sprague and Associates**; *Author of "The Masters Touch"*

"The music of Tamra's poetry will sing to your heart...the messages will lift your heart...her ministry will bless your heart...as she shares her heartfelt reflections in honor of her God-given gift."

> - **John Horton**; *Founder and President, The Leadership Forum; Atlanta, GA.*

"As I read Tamra's poetry, I can tell that she has surrendered her heart to the Lordship of Jesus Christ. She has the wonderful capacity to bring every kind of circumstance in her life to the feet of Jesus. Let her words inspire you to do the same."

> \- **Jonathan Munson**; *Worship and Music Associate; Johnson Ferry Baptist Church, Marietta, GA.*

"Tamra's poetry is an education in itself- reminding us to lean on God as she reveals how He keeps her "calm through the storms." Thank you, Tamra, for being a messenger of God's love and His never failing presence through our trials and tribulations."

> -**Kay Nielsen**; *Learning Consultant*

"Great heartfelt words- beautiful heart behind her pain- someone can benefit from reading her words."

> -**Maggie Dickhaus**; *Member, Johnson Ferry Baptist Church; Marietta, GA.*

"The lines to a favorite song say: 'Love is not in the heart to stay, for love is not love until it is given away.'" This is Tamra Cantore. She is 'The Calm Throughout Life's Storms.' Whether it is the gift of love through her poetry or the gift of her presence, she is love."

> \- **Colonel Stewart O. Davis**; *U.S. Army (retired); President and CEO of Allons Leadership, Inc.*

"Tamra Cantore is a uniquely gifted woman, setting words to poetry for God's glory. Her poems will bless you as they bless God."

> \- **Brian Hedrick**; *Minister of Instrumental Music, Johnson Ferry Baptist Church; Marietta, GA*

"Life's Storms" are something Tamra Cantore knows a lot about. She's married to a "weatherman," but no one could have predicted that Tamra would find herself fighting for herself and for others who suffer from Parkinson's disease. Tamra's poetry is grounded in reality, and lifts the reader with hope. She has reached inside for strength, and reached out to others with determination in her life as well as her writing. Her poetry speaks of both her own struggle, and her struggle for others. With simple words Tamra shares eternal truths and her deepening faith. Her poetry is a gift to the reader, and like the rainbow, a reminder that storms do end. She deepens this pastor's faith with the certainty of her own."

- **Rev. Dr. Richard L. Sheffield**; *Market Street Presbyterian Church; Lima, OH*

"REFLECTIONS," a collection of poetry by Tamra Cantore, has rested on my nightstand since she gave it to me two years ago. It's the last thing I see when I go to bed and the first thing I see each morning. Her prayers in poetry never fail to inspire me and help me remember God will never leave nor forsake me. Tamra's strong faith in the Lord is evident in her poetry. This faith allows her to turn mere words into worshipful praise of God who is the source of her strength. My favorite lines are the last two in "Elizabeth" and describe my personal feeling for Tamra. "Knowing you is a special and precious gift, it's true, and making you most beautiful, is the sweet spirit inside of you."

- **Hugh Eaton**; *Vice President (Retired); The Weather Channel, Inc.*

"Tamra's words of encouragement come from a deep well of personal courage. Her passages soothe the soul with an authentic light of hope. Her thoughts transcend time and speak universal truths that followers of any faith can find meaning in."

- **Mish Michaels**; *Meteorologist; CBS 4 Boston*

Table of Contents

Author's Notes

Turning your life over to God and trusting Him in ALL things sounds good on paper, but when we are faced with difficult times in our life, do our actions back up the faith and trust in our Lord which we have been proclaiming?

As I was approaching my 40th Birthday I learned that I had Parkinson's disease (which also afflicted both of my Grandfathers.) This debilitating neurological condition is a progressive disorder currently without a cure. With great optimism from the doctors and scientists about the likelihood of finding a cure for Parkinson's within the following 5-10 years, and with the new dopamine agonist medication which had just been approved, I was able to ignore the disease and get on with my normal routine...for a while. As my condition was worsening, we also learned that both of our children had various learning disorders ranging from ADHD to auditory processing issues to Epilepsy and Fragile X Syndrome (which is now the most diagnosed form of hereditary mental impairment.)

I was reaching the end of my rope, and I had reached a crisis of faith...would I live out the words I had been proclaiming and trust God to take control of my life including this situation? In an act of desperation, I turned it over to God and only then was I able to see my circumstance from a different perspective. It is then that I was able to receive the blessings which God had in store for me from my circumstances.

As God has promised, when He allows trials in our lives, He will provide the means for getting through them. In God's mercy, He has given the grace I need to sustain me through the challenges of each difficult day. And, beyond human understanding, I feel incredibly blessed. Not only am I able to face each day with a sense of peace that could only come from God, He has revealed my gift of poetry which has ministered so much to me and in God-sized ways, has also ministered to others.

God has slowly revealed how the path he laid for my life was specifically designed for such a time as this. Through the relationships I had nurtured during twenty-three years working in the telecommunications industry, I have been blessed with tremendous support for me and for

TEAM CANTORE, (a team which was founded specifically to raise funding for Parkinson's research.) (*See more information in the Parkinson's Unity Walk section of Resources.*)

This book of poetry is another small way in which I intend to contribute toward funding Parkinson's research. Remaining proceeds will go toward funding Fragile X research at Emory University and to support the Right from the Heart Ministries outreach in Marietta, GA. With the purchase of each book, you are helping get us one step closer to a cure.

May God Richly Bless You!
Tamra Cantore

Storm Shelter

"God is our refuge and strength, always ready to help in times of trouble."
(NLT)
- Psalm 46:1

The Sacrificial Lamb

God so loved the world, that He sent His only Son,
The Most Holy; Most High; the Anointed One.

Born to face the trials we've faced, on the pathway we have trod,
Through Jesus' life, we caught a glimpse, of the loving nature of our God.

Sent to die, not for His sins, but for the sins of all mankind,
Washing us clean from all unrighteousness; cutting us free from sins that bind.

Jesus gave His life for each one of us who asks Him to be their Lord,
His selfless and obedient act, allows our hearts to be restored.

The blood Jesus shed at Calvary, as He hung upon the cross,
Saved (and is still saving) sinners' lives which once were lost.

Satan uses seeds of shame and doubt to drag our lives back into sin,
He's still trying to build his army, but it's a war he'll never win.

When Jesus shed His blood that day, on the cross at Calvary,
It looked like Satan won the battle; but it was Jesus' victory.

The unblemished Lamb of God, was sent to pay the highest price,
He was the one and only perfect and suitable sacrifice.

On the third day, when the stone rolled back, Jesus emerged out of the grave,
And He returned to Heaven's Royal Throne to intercede for those He saves.

"I am the Good Shepherd.
The Good Shepherd lays down his life for the sheep." (NLT)
- John 10:11

Where Jesus Dwells

A house is so much more, than a structure made of wood,
It's a place where we can be ourselves, when nowhere else we could.

It's a place where we feel free to share, our deepest thoughts and fears,
Away from a judgmental world, where no one else can hear.

When we know we've made mistakes, we go there to release,
To repent for things we know were wrong and restore our sense of peace.

It's a place of refuge, after working hard all day,
It shelters us and gets us through the storms that come our way.

It's a place where we can go, to get much needed rest,
Those who enter sense the love and feel that they've been blessed.

There's a sense of comfort, when we're finally safe at home,
Even when we're by ourselves, we do not feel alone.

A wooden cross and nails were used when Jesus died for me,
When I look at my house of wood, it's Jesus that I see.

"If you make the LORD your refuge, if you make the Most High your shelter,
no evil will conquer you; no plague will come near your dwelling." (NLT)
- Psalm 91:9-10

Through Jesus Alone

Material wealth nor good works here on earth,
Can get us to heaven, or give spiritual birth.

It is simply by faith, in God's word that we trust,
His free gift is given, to each one of us.

No man or woman, who has ever lived,
Is free of sin; how could God forgive?

But in God's mercy, purely by grace,
He sent us His son, to die in our place.

As my statement of faith, I resolve to believe,
That through Jesus alone, salvation's received.

"Jesus told him, 'I am the way, the truth, and the life.
No one can come to the Father except through me." (NLT)
- John 14:6

Fear Not

Satan plays upon our fears, and our insecurities,
He wants us to begin to doubt, the truth, which we believe.

Satan tries to break our spirit, so God's work, we cannot do,
But our focus should remain on God, His promises are true.

When God lets us walk dark valleys, sometimes we feel we've lost our way,
We can call on God's almighty power; all we need to do is pray.

Wherever God may lead us, we know he goes there too,
He lifts us up, with strength to face, whatever we go through.

So, don't lose heart, or start to fall into self-pity or defeat,
By God's grace, we may boldly leave all fears at Jesus' feet.

"I command you - be strong and courageous! Do not be afraid or discouraged.
For the LORD your God is with you wherever you go." (NLT)
- Joshua 1:9

We're Not Alone

We want so very desperately, to try and understand,
How such heavy burdens, could pass through God's loving hands.

Satan tries to send his blame and doubt, in the evil game he plays,
But there's peace, not condemnation, on the path of life God's laid.

If anyone could ever know, the depth of pain we feel,
It's God, who sent His son to die, for our salvation to be sealed.

The valleys of this life are deep; we can't face them on our own,
But God, our loving Father, won't let us walk alone.

This would not have been the path we chose, but our ways are not God's
ways,
The creator of all life brings good, even from our darkest days.

Amidst the trials we're facing, praise God for what He'll do,
When we look up to God, we focus less, on what we're going through.

God has promised His believers, a future and a hope,
He'll give us peace that we can't understand, and strength for us to cope.

It's when we're at our weakest, God's mighty strength's revealed,
His light guides us through our darkest hour, and in His love we're healed.

---

*"Do not be afraid or discouraged, for the LORD is the one who goes before you.
He will be with you; He will neither fail you nor forsake you." (NLT)
- Deuteronomy 31:8*

One Prayer Away

I had always thought I knew what it meant,
To be a "Christian"; you sin – you repent.
You treat people nice; go to church on Sunday,
The Bible unused, on a shelf; on display.

But somehow I never seemed to be taught,
Salvation can't be earned or bought.
The only way (yes there's only one),
To assure your salvation is through Christ, God's Son.

Acknowledge your sins, ask Christ into your heart,
And God will give you a brand new start.
Whatever you've done, He forgives all past sins,
He gives you His Spirit as your new life begins.

For eternity, your salvation now sealed,
The true meaning of scriptures and hymns now revealed.
I thank God for opening my eyes that day,
To see that salvation was only one prayer away.

"For anyone who calls on the name of the LORD will be saved." (NLT)
-Romans 10:13

Jesus

*J*ust when you think you can't take any more,
  Beyond understanding, a sense of peace is restored.

*E*ven when life's tragedies happen to you,
  The impossible lies ahead, but you make it through.

*S*ometimes when things just aren't going your way,
  You find you're better off now than you were yesterday.

*U*nder the pressures of life and everyday stress,
  You're stopped and reminded of how much you've been blessed.

*S*o, what gives you this peace and the comfort from pain?
  Our savior, Jesus Christ; the Living God who reigns!

"I am leaving you with a gift - peace of mind and heart.
And the peace I give isn't like the peace that the world gives.
So don't be troubled or afraid." (NLT)
- John 14:27

Warnings and Advisories

"If your sinful nature controls your mind, there is death.
But if the Holy Spirit controls your mind, there is life and peace." (NLT)
- Romans 8:6

A Prayer for the New Millennium

At the end of such a historic year,
Let's pause to reflect on why we are here.
As years go by and the world's compassion grows colder,
Spreading the good news of Christ rests on our shoulders.

America, our country, has truly been blessed,
But with the evil that's thriving, Christians can't be at rest.
We have to stand up for the truth; all that's right,
This country won't mend 'til Christians stand up and fight.

Though we each were born to this world of sin,
Our greatest defense is God's Spirit within.
Satan will come knocking in our weakest hour,
But with Jesus in our hearts, he has no power.

We stray off course, for in our sin we cannot see,
But God's given us His Spirit, to lead us faithfully.
We can't take back moments in life to relive,
But what comfort and hope God's promises give.

Through Jesus, salvation is God's gift to you,
Putting faith in our Lord is all we need do.
God sent us His son at such a great cost,
Jesus laid down his life so not one would be lost.

May the truth of God's Word, in your heart be sealed,
He will comfort and guide you, when to His will you yield.
So cast the load of your burdens onto the Lord,
With faith in Jesus, peace will be your reward.

---

*"For this, O LORD, I will praise you among the nations;
I will sing joyfully to your name." (NLT)*
- Samuel 22:50

If You Knew What You Were Missing

When I think of what you're missing, it sometimes makes me cry,
Blessings God's prepared for you, are lost as you rush by.

You keep searching for someone or thing, to make your life complete,
When the field of joy God's grown for you, is right beneath your feet.

Jesus died upon the cross, for sin and death to be destroyed,
It's God's love, that fills our hearts, where we once felt a void.

I pray that you'll discover, where true happiness is found,
When you surrender to the will of God, great blessings will abound.

When Jesus dwells within our hearts, salvation's our reward,
And a peace, beyond our hopes and dreams, through Jesus Christ the Lord.

"So I pray that God, who gives you hope,
will keep you happy and full of peace as you believe in him.
May you overflow with hope through the power of the holy spirit." (NLT)
~ Romans 15:13

Just a Fleeting Moment

Just a fleeting moment, our life is here on earth,
How precious are the memories; more than riches are they worth.

We never want to squander, the brief moments of our lives,
The ones, who matter most to us, are right before our eyes.

Each time we've stopped to tell the special people that we know,
How much their lives have blessed us, our blessings overflow.

We never are quite ready, when God calls a loved one home,
But He's always there to hold us, when we can't stand on our own.

God calls some before the others; why?; we'll never understand,
But we know our loving Father, has got a perfect plan,

In God's almighty mercy, we feel His peace amidst our pain,
And we're comforted in knowing, that our loss is Heaven's gain!

LORD, remind me how brief my time on earth will be.
Remind me that my days are numbered,
and that my life is fleeing away." (NLT)
- Psalm 39:4

Mommy!

When I'm busy and I hear my name...
for the 20th time; I go insane.
"Use your words, and tell me, now!
"I'd help you, but I don't know how."

There are times, it seems, that nothing pleases,
the whining and complaining never ceases.
"Did you hear what I said?" (as my volume grows),
Only on the third of three chances, their listening skill shows!

When they disobey, the threats begin,
"There'll be consequences, if you do that again!"
Sending kids to their room, no longer works well,
A computer and toys punishment? (They can't really tell.)

"No sweets after dinner; tonight, no TV,"
(I know it was never this hard raising me!)
When I'd do something wrong, very quickly I'd see,
The look of disappointment; that's how Dad punished me.

I wonder what's wrong with these kids today?
(Or is it my blaming finger, that's turned the wrong way?)
Is the reason they call me as much as they do,
Because I'm so focused, on what "I've" got to do?

Kids are smart (and they always know how, it seems,)
To get the attention they want, by whatever means.
What do I get, for completing that long list of "things,"
Compared to the joy on a face that a Mother's hug brings.

Our time here is precious; I'm not sure that shows,
I get bogged down in the midst of my daily woes,
Lord, change my heart so my life reflects,
My love for these gifts, with which I've been blessed.

---

*"My child, listen to me and do as I say, and you will have a long, good life.
I will teach you wisdom's ways and lead you in straight paths." (NLT)*
- Proverbs 4:10-11

It's About Time

We never seem to have much time,
We rush ahead, but stay behind.

Our calendars; full of things to do,
It'll be next week, 'till I've got time for you.

In our multi-task world, we don't slow down,
To make someone smile, when we see a frown.

So focused on "me," we don't take time,
When others try to share, what's on their mind.

What kind of message do we send,
When we can't stop and listen to a friend?

Our time is "Precious" (we've made that clear,)
Do our actions speak "words" we want others to hear?

Time shared with others, is time well spent,
It's an expression of love and encouragement.

Give the gift of time, to someone else, today,
You'll find moments are **most** precious, when you give them away.

"My days are swifter than a weaver's shuttle flying back and forth." (NLT)
- Job 7:6a

Words

Words can make you laugh; make you mad or make you cry,
They can be a shield of comfort; or very empty when they lie.

Words can be a melody; defining beauty, bringing joy,
Or, can be so curt and ugly, with a motive to destroy.

Words can tell the tale; how someone else has fallen short,
Casting insults, couched as jokes, and people laugh at the retort.

Words can add another burden, to the stressful life you live,
Can relieve your heavy heart, when they say that they forgive.

Sometimes it's even better, for Words to not be said at all,
You say you care, just being there; as your own tears may fall.

Words can be a deadly weapon; they can cut just like a knife,
But when used with care and grace, can bring love into a life.

So, ask yourself this question, "Am I proud of what I say,
Would my Words feel like a blessing, if someone spoke to me this way?"

Words can be so very powerful; don't underestimate,
The earth, the sky and all mankind; with Words did God create!

"A person's words can be life giving water;
words of true wisdom are as refreshing as a bubbling brook." (NLT)
- Proverbs 18:4

Today's Prayer

As we go our separate ways,
To work, to school, or out to play;
Know that, when you're away from home,
You never are, really, all alone,

Our love goes with you, no matter where,
You know if you need us, we'll always be there.
And never forget, If you're sad or scared,
God always listens, when we ask Him in prayer.

Remember the things, we have taught you to do,
Treat others the way, you want them to treat you.
Through Jesus' example, you know right from wrong,
To guide and remind us, He sends His Spirit along.

So wherever you go, and whatever you do,
Make Jesus proud, to be there with you.
And when you're safe, back home at rest,
Thank God for this day, with which you've been blessed.

---

*"Once Jesus had been out praying, one of his disciples came to him
and said, "LORD, teach us to pray just as John taught his disciples."" (NLT)
~ Luke 11:1*

Have We Made a Difference?

In my middle years, when I should be at my best,
Comes news so unexpected; I never would have guessed.

Parkinson's?! Not me! (Even one doctor told me so.)
"You surely couldn't have it; you'd be the youngest that I know!"

But it started sinking in, telling friends and family,
Watching their tears and disbelief; "you're too young; this couldn't be!"

The reality of symptoms, can no longer be disguised,
Seeing pain and disappointment, in your spouse's eyes.

Feeling the effects; what this condition takes away,
Sports you once had mastered, now more difficult to play.

Dressing Barbies makes me crazy, I can't brush my daughter's hair,
The kids wonder why you're shaking; hand control no longer there.

Knowing that without a cure, the symptoms magnify,
There could be a sense of hopelessness; just simply wondering why?

But God promises believers, He won't leave us alone,
He never will forsake us, to face life's trials on our own.

His timing is always perfect, this couldn't be more true,
My news comes on the brink, of a major medical breakthrough.

To those controlling funding, to ensure a cure is found,
Know, the kind of impact you could have; is historically profound!

Give prayerful consideration, to the decisions that you make,
Understand the sense of urgency; over 1 million lives are now at stake.

What's the legacy that we'll leave, looking back on this decade?
Did we fund research and find the cure; what kind of difference have we made?

"With God's help we will do mighty things..." (NLT)
- Psalm 60:12

Search My Heart

Even in this high-tech world, I have too much to do,
I get so many e-mails, I don't have time to speak to you.

Keep talking, I can listen, while I do three other things,
You might just want to speed it up, before my cell phone rings.

Please start the game without me (who knows how long I'll be?)
These on-line deals have deadlines, so they get top priority.

I find so much information; another project's on my mind,
Wait until this search downloads; (who knows just what I'll find?)

I find myself just surfing in the middle of the night,
Chasing information; non-essential to my life.

There is so much information, whether it's of use to me or not,
I can't believe the time I've spent when I look up at the clock.

Time spent on-line's increasing; it's hard to stop it once you start,
Am I spending just as much spare time on matters of the heart?

How precious is each moment that you've given just to me,
LORD help me use this precious gift of time, much more carefully.

"Search me, O God, and know my heart; test me and know my thoughts." (NLT)
- Psalm 139:23

Without Christ

Without Christ, constant chaos controls how we live our life,
We feel hopeless; weighed down by our trials and our strife.

Without Christ, there's resentment; we pay sins back with more sins,
We're indignant about what WE deserve as we strive so hard to "Win".

Without Christ, we're self-centered; our needs take top priority,
When things don't go the way we planned, tempers flare so easily.

Without Christ, we're easy targets in Satan's game meant to destroy,
He wants to see us doubt our faith, and rob us of life's joy.

Without Christ, we're nothing; but in Christ we can do all things,
He gives us strength to cope and joy-filled hope whatever this life brings.

"Yes, I am the vine; you are the branches.
Those who remain in me, and I in them, will produce much fruit.
For apart from me you can do nothing." (NLT)
- John 15:5

Am I Thankful?

Am I thankful for the many gifts, God's given in His grace,
Do I focus on His promises, amidst the trials that I face?

Am I thankful for things big and small, He does for me each day?
Do I thank Him for the gift of life; do I praise Him when I pray?

Am I thankful for my friends, do I choose words carefully,
Do I show the Lord's compassion, and serve others selflessly?

Am I thankful for the blessing, of a loving family?
Do I let go of daily stresses, so they're my top priority?

Am I thankful for this country, and the blessings of this land?
Do I wait patiently? God will reveal, what it is that He has planned.

I'm thankful for all these gifts, but what do my actions say?
Let each new day with which I'm blessed, be my "thanks giving" day!

"Give thanks to the LORD, for he is good!
His faithful love endures forever." (NLT)
- 1 Chronicles 16:34

The Perfect Gift

To find the perfect gift to give, (no matter what the cost),
The spirit of the season, often times gets lost.

A truly perfect gift, can't be found in any store,
It's not "his" brand new golf club, or the sweater "she" adores.

As you were thinking what to buy, and making out your list,
Did you include a gift for Jesus, or was He someone that you missed?

The perfect gift for Jesus can't be wrapped beneath the tree,
It's His light that lives within us, so that others clearly see.

It's that special something; a part of us that we can give,
That creates a treasured memory; held dear, as long as one may live.

With generosity in giving (not without some sacrifice),
The gift will be a true reflection, of the joy that's in your life.

As precious as our gifts are, it's by God's grace we receive,
The perfect gift of Jesus; salvation for all who will believe!

"Every good and perfect gift is from above,
coming down from the Father of the heavenly lights.." (NLT)
- James 1:17

Rainy Days

"We are pressed on every side by troubles, but we are not crushed and broken.
We are perplexed, but we don't give up and quit." (NLT)
- Psalm 46:1

Take it to the Lord

We get knocked down, and question, why our challenges have grown,
But it's taken **this**, for us to realize, we can't make it on our own.

God will be there waiting, when life brings us to our knees,
He wants for us to come in prayer; He restores our sense of peace.

God knows everything we're facing, and what's coming down the road,
He's always there beside us, helping carry our heavy load.

If we trust in God the Father, we have to give it **all** to Him,
Every problem, big and small, which troubles us within.

He'll reveal the glory of His plan (so hard for us to see,)
He desires us to prosper, and to live abundantly.

Even in the worst of times, our joy can be restored,
God heals us with a loving heart; all He asks you for is yours!

"When I had lost all hope, I turned my thoughts once more to the LORD.
And my earnest prayer went out to you in your holy Temple." (NLT)
~ Jonah 2:7

Letting Go

I proclaim, that I strive, to follow God's will,
But is it earth's desires that lead me still?

Does it matter; no world defined "success" remains?
When all I need, comes from the God who reigns.

I blame it on others, but am I the one?
Is my worth defined by work, or by God's only Son?

God, you are speaking to me, am I listening to you?
It's become very clear, what you want me to do.

But, am I able, to take such a leap?
To trust in God; His promises to keep?

Why should I worry; what could be lost?
The eternal rewards, are well worth the cost.

Though my heart is willing; doubt has taken its toll,
Lord, may I resist earthly pride, and let you take control.

"Trust in the LORD with all your heart;
do not depend on your own understanding.
Seek his will in all you do, and he will direct your paths." (NLT)
- Proverbs 3:5-6

Can We See God?

If we look, can we see God, in our daily lives?
He's working all around us, though we don't often realize.

We can't look upon God's face, until we're called before His throne,
But, He reveals His love to us, while in our earthly home.

God's in the smile that greets you, when life's been difficult all day,
When the spot on the x-ray disappears, He's made it go away.

Though your car cannot be salvaged (it was totaled in the crash.)
You live to tell the story, God got you through without a scratch

You are running very late for work and the toilet overflows,
A bulletin comes on TV to say roads are closed because of snow.

You wouldn't normally have been there, but your meeting time was switched,
So you were there to get the call that your child just might need a stitch.

The tornado thunders down the street; damage you thought you'd never see,
And right next door some other houses stand just as they used to be.

If we just stop for a minute from living at such a hectic pace,
We get just a glimpse of God's awesome power and beauty of His grace.

"Be silent, and know that I am God!
I will be honored by every nation.
I will be honored throughout the world." (NLT)
- Psalm 46:10

"My" Will Be Done

You've decided on the path you'll take; the time is drawing near,
But, God's laid these words upon my heart; I have to let you hear.

Rushing a decision, with such great permanence,
Adds complications (to a complex life) of great significance.

What you don't know is what hurts you; (will advisors' words sink in,)
Before you've jumped too quickly, and hard lessons of life begin?

It's not a random person, or just a few that see,
The same concerns have surfaced, from many (not just me.)

God uses prayers, circumstances, church and His Holy Word,
To speak to us and guide us; if we listen, He'll be heard.

Which signs are you reading as you travel this fast track?
When you rush to make decisions, there is no turning back.

Postponing things and waiting, may seem too hard to do,
But it's time and actions (not just words) that reveals the truth to you.

If this truly is the will of God, time will make your path more clear,
When you follow, where He leads; great blessings shall appear.

"Show me the path where I should walk, O LORD;
point out the right road for me to follow." (NLT)
- Psalm 25:4

He Cares for You with Love

Even though, we'd like to think, our lives are in our control,
God reminds us His own way, that it's not our role.

Whatever is in store for us; even though we cannot see,
We know God's plan is perfect; we can trust Him faithfully.

So even in those moments, when it's hard to understand,
The pain and why you're suffering; we know God's in command.

The God who made the flowers grow, and all the stars above,
Knows the plan He's got for you; and cares for you with love.

"And we know that God causes everything to work together
for the good of those people who love God
and are called according to his purpose for them." (NLT)
- Romans 8:28

Quiet Moments

In my quiet moments, during the late night hours,
I pray we find the love, which used to be ours.
Time spent frequently together, is just a memory,
The pace of our lives, not what it used to be.

Facing many interruptions, when, at last, we're eye to eye,
Our communication suffers; it should be no wonder why.
With a crazy working schedule and activities on the rise,
We make time for kids and errands, but our own is compromised.

Our patience tends to suffer and tempers sometimes flare,
But somewhere deep within our hearts, we know we really care.
It seems no matter what we do, or how hard we both have tried,
Completion of all those "things to do" is never realized.

We're caught up in the quicksand that our hectic life demands,
But Jesus waits to rescue us with His outstretched hand.
Things impossible for us, are not a problem for the Lord,
If we trust with faith in Him, peace and love will be restored.

"...my nights were filled with joyful songs.
I search my soul and think about the difference now." (NLT)
- Psalm 77:76

Forget You Not

For all the things I haven't done; each Birthday that I've missed,
It's not that I forgot you or that I crossed you off my list!

As much as I would like to do, all the things I used to do,
My list keeps growing daily, of the things I can't get to.

Each day I've such few hours when my hands are working fine,
So many things I want to do, can't be done in that short time.

My heart breaks just to think of how I've been so out of touch,
I love my friends and family, so very, very much!

You're on my mind quite often, even though it doesn't show,
So many notes I should have sent, but I have to let it go.

So, in advance, I'll ask forgiveness, for the next thing I let slide,
(My symptoms always worsen, when guilt and stress build up inside.)

While others will still question, why I don't do what I should do,
Please know, you're always in my thoughts and my prayers are with you too!

---

*"Then Peter came to him and asked, "Lord, how often should I forgive
someone who sins against me? Seven times?"
"No!" Jesus replied, "seventy times seven!" (NLT)
~ Matthew 18:21-23*

He Dries Our Tears

Christianity gives us no guarantee,
That troubles won't come to you or to me.
In fact, suffering comes to each one of us,
But our lives depend on the God we trust.

Make no mistake, God has a plan,
Though sometimes we can't understand.
But in His time God will reveal,
Through His word; He helps us heal.

God promises us He is always there,
Stay close to Him through faith and prayer.
"He sets (us) free from all (our) fears"
He gives us hope; He dries our tears.

"I prayed to the LORD, and he answered me, freeing me from all my fears." (NLT)
- Psalm 34:4

Rainbows

"I have placed my rainbow in the clouds.
It is the sign of my permanent promise to you and to all the earth." (NLT)
- Genesis 9:13

At Times Like This

At times like this, I find myself,
Pulling your picture down off the shelf.

I see your eyes and start to cry,
Memories fill my mind from times gone by.

Overflowing with both smiles and tears,
Cherished moments we shared throughout the years.

The life you lived, made it clear to see,
Your love for Jesus, and His love for me.

You revealed God's Words of joy and hope,
Of strength found in Christ, when we can't cope.

You left us your legacy, founded in Christ,
You modeled the way, we all long to live life.

Now the Heavenly Father, reaches out for my hand,
He whispers, "all things work together for good, in my plan."

The warmth of God's love now shines up from your face,
And peace pours down on me, in God's shower of grace.

"There is a time for everything, a season for every activity under heaven.
A time to be born and a time to die." (NLT)
- Ecclesiastes 3:1-2

The Blessings Fell Like Rain

It wasn't a day of sunshine or blue skies,
But no one would let the rain be it's demise.
Family and friends, from times past (and some new),
Equally committed, to what they're there to do.

With compassion and friendship, sincerity and love,
There were tears; there was laughter and many wet hugs.
The encouragement offered by each person there,
Helped strengthen the afflicted, as they sensed such great care.

Many, came to honor a loved one they'd lost,
Knowing, research, will keep others from paying this cost.
And some, living with the struggles of this horrid disease,
Uniting as one voice, with their funding pleas.

Much of the challenge, is to let people know,
How close the cure is, and where dollars go.
Scientists are passionate, about finding a cure,
They're so close, that with funding, a solution is sure.

Incurable, is no longer, how they view this disease,
It's a chance for millions of lives to set free.
The progress toward finding a cure gives us hope,
But the funding still needed is quite large in scope.

There was incredible support from some industry friends,
And The Weather Channel exposure, we all must commend.
When I start to wonder why this disease came my way,
I see the path God's been laying in my life for this day.

I sit back, in awe, as I fight this disease,
Watching God even working through people like me.
When I'm feeling defeated and zest for life has been drained,
I'm refreshed by the blessings God sends with the rain.

"The LORD will send rain at the proper time
from his rich treasury in the heavens to bless all the work you do."
- Deuteronomy 28:12

I'm on my way to Heaven

I'm on my way to Heaven; life on earth goes quickly by,
Give thanks for every breath you take; they're gifts from God on high.

I'm on my way to Heaven, part of God's plan; in His time,
Only He knows when He'll call us home; the choice is His, not mine.

I'm on my way to Heaven, for my loved ones, say a prayer,
Broken hearts find a sense of peace, when safely in God's care.

I'm on my way to Heaven, but until my mission's done,
God uses trials here on earth, to glorify His Son.

I'm on my way to Heaven, until my final day,
I'll be a witness for the Lord; He is the only way.

I'm on my way to Heaven, I will not be afraid,
There's a place prepared for me, through the debt that Jesus paid.

I'm on my way to Heaven; please don't cry for me,
In Heaven; no pain or suffering for all eternity.

I'm on my way to Heaven, as promised in God's Word,
As a believer, in Jesus Christ, salvation is assured!

"He will remove all of their sorrows,
and there will be no more death or sorrow or crying or pain.
For the old world and its evils are gone forever." (NLT)
~ Revelation 21:4

Lady Liberty

In the name, of freedom, she stands,
To welcome the tired and poor to this land.
A symbol of liberty for all who come in,
The past left behind; a new chance to begin.

An awesome and inspiring sight,
Standing proudly by day; shining brightly by night.
Overflowing with such great pride in this land,
One nation under God, united we stand.

An overwhelming burden, she now bears,
Mourning losses; which nations around the world shared.
No longer, the majestic skyline she sees,
But destruction meant to bring, our land, to its knees.

The one thing, such evil, failed to consider,
Was that this heinous act, might just, draw us together.
We fell to our knees, but to worship our King,
To praise Him for the glory and justice He'll bring.

We gathered to pray; for comfort; for peace
For our sorrow, our leaders; for the horror to cease.
To give thanks for the blessings of this land where we live,
For failing to stand up for His truth; God, forgive.

Now her tears are changing from sorrow to pride,
As the fear for our Lord, this great nation revives.
As reverence for God strengthens from shore to shore,
So too will His blessings on our land be restored.

---

*"Then if my people that are called by my name will humble themselves
and pray and seek my face and turn from their wicked ways,
I will hear from heaven and will forgive their sins and heal their land." (NLT)*
- 2 Chronicles 7:14

What's a Girl to do?

When the time for retirement, finally comes,
And the day to day work routine is done,
Deadlines and responsibilities, now through,
You're asking yourself, "What's a girl to do?

Will I wake up wondering, "should I get out of bed?"
"With no plans for the day, it's getting bored that I dread!"
"I can't imagine a morning, not occupying "my space."
"I can accomplish so much, when I run at that pace."

Then, you sit back and ponder, the things you've let go,
Getting to work by 8; whether rain, sleet or snow.
Going to work, (even when, you didn't feel good,)
Because work's piling up (though your peers understood.)

At work, we are striving to all "make the grade."
We cherish recognition and the accolades.
But as precious as your "work life" moments may be,
In the end, are these moments, top priority?

Then, think about things you WILL get to do,
Helping out with grand kids, when their mom needs you to.
Visiting friends, you've not seen for quite a long time,
Doing that simple, kind gesture, that's been on your mind.

Co-workers will miss seeing, your bright, smiling face,
Finding a replacement is tricky, (but, employees can be replaced!)
To your family, there's only one person who'll do,
It's simply no contest. Only you fill those shoes.

After creating the world, even God needed rest!
Your faith in his path for your life will be blessed,
The time that you'll have to give family and friends,
Will be MOST rewarding to you in the end!

"Can all your worries add a single moment to your life? Of course not." (NLT)
- Matthew 6:27

Rising Above

God put you together; it's part of His plan,
United; now one; as only He can.
You've been blessed with each other for a lifetime to share,
You begin this new journey, under God's loving care.

For love to stand the test of time,
God's Word is the blueprint; marriage defined.
Always working together as one,
Compassion for each other, and love for His Son.

Accepting differences; allowing imperfection,
Spending time together; with love and affection.
Husband and wife; as God made from the start,
Letting nothing on earth ever pull you apart.

God's there to guide you, and hears when you pray,
He joined you together; He'll show you the way.
It takes true commitment and a lot of love,
But a union grounded in Christ, will always "rise above."

---

*"For the Christian wife brings holiness to her marriage,
and the Christian husband brings holiness to his marriage.
Otherwise, your children would not have a godly influence,
but now they are set apart for him." (NLT)*
- 1 Corinthians 7:14

The Blessing of My Burden

We make our mark on many lives, down the road of life God's laid.
Though we seldom ever get to hear, of the impact we have made.

Though fondly they remember, many don't take time to share,
How much your life has touched them; to express how much they care.

If not but for my burden, I may have otherwise not known,
How others view the harvest, from the seeds my life has sown.

---

*"They weep as they go to plant their seed,
but they sing as they return with the harvest." (NLT)*
- Psalm 126:6

When Angels Pray

When Angels gather, God is near,
Their humble prayers, He wants to hear.
Facing issues alone, just can't compare,
To the comfort of the Angels' prayers.

The Angels share a special love,
And trusting faith in God above.
When under the weight of our burdens bound,
The Angels' prayers are all around.

If we stumble or if we stray,
The Angels' prayers aren't far away.
When we think we can't face one more day,
The Lord gives us strength, when Angels pray.

Whether joyful, or when trials come,
The Angels praise God and His Holy Son.
Angels lift our prayers up, one by one,
That in our lives, God's will be done.

What a blessing that the Angels care,
We find peace amidst the Angels' prayers.
How precious the privilege, that we may,
Join with the Angels, when they pray.

---

*"The earnest prayer of a righteous person
has great power and wonderful results." (NLT)*
- James 5:16b

Snowflakes

"I was wonderfully and fearfully made." (NLT)
- Psalm 119:39

God's Masterpiece

The artist of our life is God; creator of all things,
He made the beauty of the earth; He calms the storms that this life brings.

God designed the plans for each of us; every child, special and unique;
Only He sees the finished work of art, before our life's complete.

There's not one part of life's portrait, that wasn't drawn by God's own
hands
Everything that this life brings, happens at His Word's command.

He paints the colors of our joy and hope in shades that are so bright,
Reflecting truth of His Holy Word, which turns darkness into light.

With each stroke of his mighty hand, the details, He fills in,
He reveals the path He's laid for us, on the road away from sin.

The price for this work of art's been paid; it's our hearts, God wants
released,
So He may unveil, our life in Christ; another masterpiece!

"Then God looked over all he had made and saw that it was excellent in every way."
(NLT)
- Genesis 1:31

Not One More Minute

As I stood and I spoke to a friend today,
it was hard to find words or know what to say.
In two short years he had lost Mom, now Dad,
it was painful to watch him so terribly sad.

His biggest regret, he said with remorse;
He just hadn't stopped from his normal day's course,
To go see his Dad, since what was the hurry?
Much to do; he seemed fine; so why even worry?

"And now," he said with a tear in his eye,
"I keep asking myself, and I wish I knew why,
Why I didn't go, and speak to my Dad.
And now he is gone; I sure wish I had."

"He has been there for me, so unselfishly,
I admired him so, and hoped I would be,
At his side, like we were when Mom passed away.
But, I was home when Dad went to Heaven that day."

You can't take those moments back to relive,
But what comfort and hope God's promises give.
For whosoever, believes in his son,
A victory over death has already been won.

Looking down from above, he is smiling with pride,
As the love from his son flows from deep down inside.
And even though he never spoke the words,
His message to Dad was clearly heard.

My friend's story, to me, has been quite profound.
Though you know how I feel without hearing a sound,
Not one more minute, could I let go,
Without saying how much I love you Dad, (you know!)

"Honor your father and mother.
Then you will live a long, full life in the land the LORD your God will give you."
(NLT)
- Exodus 20:12

Grandma

Such fun I had, when I was small,
Playing at "Grandma's" was always a ball!
From dress up clothes, to games outside;
To the antique organ I played with pride.

When on occasion, I'd bring a friend,
All who came, were welcomed in.
She modeled acceptance; she modeled love,
Leaving judgment of others, to God above.

She focused most on others' needs,
No matter what her own might be.
Earrings on and always dressed,
And a sweet little smile to greet her guests.

It's no wonder Grandpa loved her so,
She was a blessing to anyone she'd get to know.
With a large giving heart (though her frame was quite small),
To me, my Grandma was biggest of all!

---

*"Dear children, let us stop just saying we love each other;
let us really show it by our actions." (NLT)*
- 1 John 3:18

Someday, Grandpa

You are a very kind and gentle man,
And for things you value, you take a stand.

Doing what's right, is always your way,
With a stellar work ethic (not found much today.)

You have shared your time so generously,
At work, at church and with your family.

For you, there couldn't have been a calling higher,
Than to care for Grandma, your heart's desire.

You're known for your fairness and integrity,
And a heart to serve others, selflessly.

I hope someday that others may see,
Some of you, Grandpa, when they look at me.

---

*"Show your fear of God by standing up in the presence of elderly people
and showing respect for the aged." (NLT)*
- Leviticus 19:32

Elizabeth

Elizabeth means "God's Oath", a perfect name for you,
You show your love and your compassion, in everything you do.

God knew what He was doing; when He designed your role to play,
You truly are a blessing, to those you meet along the way.

You have a pleasant inner peace, which others clearly see,
Patiently helping others, when you see someone in need.

.And though I keep on trying, you are, the way I hope to be,
God's Word is sealed upon your heart; you live life gracefully.

Knowing you, is one of my, most precious gifts, it's true,
And making you, most beautiful, is the sweet Spirit inside of you.

"But you are not controlled by your sinful nature.
You are controlled by the spirit if you have the spirit of God living in you." (NLT)
- Romans 8:9

Christina, Ballerina

Ballerinas, dainty, dancing; such a sight to see,
Angels float as if on clouds, in perfect harmony.

Lovely little girls, have devoted so much time,
Learning each new step and jump; playing it over in their mind.

Elegance and beauty (not just from what they wear),
Radiant smiles, light up the stage, with each new skill they share.

Instructors proudly watch, knowing their work is now complete,
Not much compares, to the joy, of those little dancing feet.

Applause erupts; dancers exit, gracefully (as they came),
Such fond memories they'll take with them; they are forever changed.

"Praise his name with dancing..." (NLT)
- Psalm 149:3

Henry

We celebrate the life, of someone who,
Boasts not of his successes (as we'd all like to do.)

All over the world, God's Word he has shared,
His wife and his family, he serves with great care.

His passion for Jesus is never at rest,
Those of us honored to know him, have truly been blessed.

No one will ever be (nor have they been yet,)
As righteous as Jesus, but he's as close as you get.

We won't see God's face, until our life here is through,
But when I picture God's face, Henry, I picture you!

---

*"...as the spirit of the LORD works within us,
we become more and more like him and reflect his glory even more." (NLT)
~ 2 Corinthians 3:18*

Bettie

We want to give Bettie, the thanks she deserves,
For the wonderful way, that she faithfully serves.
She spends hours preparing, for the lessons she shares,
She may say, "Sorry, I'm preaching," but none of us care!

Her life, has not been a life lived without pain,
She finds peace, in the knowledge, that it's her Savior who reigns.
With every ounce of energy, that she has to give,
She's in steadfast pursuit, of a heart just like His.

Though she's petite in stature, she's enormous in grace,
She models a life, with priorities, properly placed.
So full of God's spirit, her joy overflows,
His light shining brightly in her; wherever she goes.

She leads her army of "Angels," toward an abundant life,
As we learn, to abide, in our Lord Jesus Christ.
Wherever you have come from; no matter what you're going through,
She makes sure you know, without a doubt, that Jesus died for you.

She tells us, we're the only "Bible" some people ever read,
God can use your life, when lived in Christ, to set more people free.
She challenges us, to know more personally, the Love of Jesus Christ,
Not just to read His Holy Words, but to apply them to our life.

She warns us, that our words will be so hollow, and will lead us to defeat,
If our actions are not right in line, with the words you hear us speak.
She warns that Satan is a prowler, seeking ways to make us weak,
Put on your righteous armor; Christ has already handed him defeat.

Bettie comforts us, when we feel, down trod,
In a big hug from Bettie, you feel the presence of God.
She lets each person know, just how much she cares,
If you know Bettie Holley, you know you're bathed with her prayers.

Her life's rooted in Christ; the life-giving vine,
The fruits of the Spirit, through her life; intertwined.
Her life's a shining example of "living the Word,"
We long to have, in our hearts, what she has in hers.

---

*"When the Holy Spirit controls our lives,
he will produce this kind of fruit in us:
love, joy, peace, patience, kindness, goodness,
faithfulness, gentleness, and self-control." (NLT)
- Galatians 5:22-23*

There's Always Hope

John had always been here, tracking each wave off the coast.
No one knew more about hurricanes (though I never heard him boast.)
The passion with which he did his work, has always been respected,
Accolades; the list is long, of awards which he's accepted.

Though John accomplished more, than ten other men could do,
When compliments started flowing, he'd turn conversations back on you.
He was such a kind and humble man and so giving of himself,
A mentor to so many; sharing knowledge of such wealth.

How much we all depended, on his insight and expertise,
We admired him, and grew to love, both he and sweet Bernice.
John was a model of commitment, to both work and family,
No one ever had to question, what were his priorities.

He brought strong confidence (with wisdom) to decipher any storm,
It was his singular mission, to keep people out of harm.
We were so blessed to know John; now, it's hard for us to cope,
But with memories stored within our hearts, we know there's always Hope!

"But those who exalt themselves will be humbled
and those who humble themselves will be exalted." (NLT)
- Matthew 23:12

More Than Meets the Eye

As an actor, Michael has such broad appeal,
He depicts his characters with passionate zeal.
He's endearing and funny; quite a charming guy,
But when it comes to Michael, there's more than meets the eye.

He reluctantly jumped into the PD fight,
He felt too much focus on him just wouldn't be right.
But it became clear over time what a difference he'd make,
To impact funding for research, if he'd use his name sake.

Michael used respect and influence he's built through the years,
To enlist the support of his Hollywood peers.
His Foundation was established and their goals were set,
Quickly earning kudos for achievements others had never met.

Michael leads his Foundation, he's not just a "pretty face,"
He authored the strategy for how they'd help win this race.
Testifying before Congress was, for him a new role,
He's helped open doors to the people with funding control.

Getting the private sector and our political machine,
Working together toward a cure was something we'd never seen.
Many pilot studies received funding once his plans were in place,
He wasn't about to just bet on one horse in the race.

When you meet him in person, the qualities you see,
Are the same ones that drew you to him on TV.
As Michael shakes your hand, he looks you straight in the face,
He wants to hear from others running in the same race.

We all count on Michael, but he needs encouragement too,
There's a bond; an understanding of what each other goes through.
Amidst the whirlwind around him, he keeps his focus on you,
And with a hug says; "hold me up, and I'll hold you up too."

He has given generously of his time and his wealth,
But not just to find a cure for himself.
It's not about just curing Michael, you see,
He's fighting for each person who has this disease.

"God has given each of us the ability to do certain things well...
If your gift is to encourage others, do it!
If you have money, share it generously.
If God has given you leadership ability,
take the responsibility seriously." (NLT)
- Matthew 23:12

Sunny Skies

"Always be full of joy in the Lord. I say it again – rejoice!" (NLT)
- Phillipians 4:4-5

For The Beauty Of The Earth

I sit and wait for the sun to rise,
The others have not yet opened their eyes.
Across the dark sky, I see shooting stars race,
I'm in awe of my God who put each one in place.

The horizon is brightening with the new morning sun,
Blessings of another new day have begun.
Each time my eyes close and open once more,
New colors emerge that weren't there before.

The fog winds in and out of each mountain top,
The grassy knoll's damp from the morning dew drops,
Deer search through the dawn for something to eat,
Then a bird breaks the silence with a song that's so sweet.

From the towering mountains to dainty flowers of spring,
My Father in Heaven created all things.
Like the warmth of the sun which now covers my face,
I bask in the beauty of these gifts of God's grace!

"This is the LORD's doing, and it is marvelous to see.
This is the day that the LORD has made.
We will rejoice and be glad in it." (NLT)
- Psalm 118:23-24

Friendship's Blessing

Through you, dear friend, I've learned first hand,
What Jesus meant by His command.

Love one another (even when not deserved),
give unselfishly, with a heart to serve.

Without hesitation, you've always been there,
Your kind heart and compassion, clearly show that you care.

When I make a mistake (as I often do),
I can count on the truth and forgiveness from you.

You are more like a sister, than friend to me,
You're trusted with things, I won't let others see.

There is not enough money, or words to show,
What a blessing you are, for me to know.

---

*"There are friends who destroy each other,
but a real friend sticks closer than a brother." (NLT)*
~ Proverbs 18:24

God's Miracle Of Birth

From the day this child was made, by the grace of God's great love,
Your lives would never be the same; what a blessing from above.

In anticipation, there's apprehension and great joy,
It doesn't make a difference, if it's a girl or it's a boy.

Just to see ten little fingers and ten tiny little toes...
You wonder if her eyes are yours; will he have his Daddy's nose?

Then comes the day you've waited for; a precious gift of life,
Little things you may complain about, now seen in a new light.

Oh how overwhelming, from the first time that you touch,
To learn it's even possible, to love someone so much.

Only now, you're really able to fully understand,
How much your Mother loves you, as you're holding this small hand.

Nothing else, I could imagine, can come close to being worth,
The joy and the great wonder, of God's miracle of birth.

---

*"For the life of every living thing is in his hand,
and the breath of all humanity." (NLT)*
- Job 12:10

Heaven Sent An Angel

Heaven sent an angel, to help me make it through,
You always sense, when I need help (and know just what to do.)

Unselfishly, you set aside, your own priorities,
To help, to listen, to give advice and take the load off me.

Your support means, much more to me, than you could ever know,
Even when I'm at my worst, you smile and let it go.

Though change is always constant, on one thing I can depend,
No matter what, when I need help, I always have a friend.

I have been your mentor, I've heard some people say,
But, I'm the one who was most blessed, when God sent you my way.

---

*"For the angel of the Lord guards all who fear him,
and he rescues them." (NLT)
- Psalms 34:7*

Steamboat

It's a quaint western town that welcomes you in,
(Not like some other places we've been!)

The scenery's tremendous; there's good food and good wine,
But much more than that, the people are so kind.

They always make you feel right at home,
There's lots to do as a group or if out on your own.

They treat you like family and welcome you in,
They're there to guide you as each new adventure begins.

It's all about families; a great place for kids too,
There is so much for folks of all ages to do.

They welcome beginners and challenge the best,
The crisp mountain air gives you a great night of rest.

For winter vacations, or for summer fun,
Steamboat has proven to be number one.

We're sad our vacation has come to an end,
We came here as strangers, but we're leaving as friends.

"Upright citizens bless this city and make it prosper..." (NLT)
- Proverbs 11:11

Joyful In Jesus

There are many on earth, who don't understand,
The peace that's found, living under God's command.

When you give your heart, and life, to the Lord,
You'll realize the blessings, in your name, God has stored.

God's love, is like nothing, you'll find here on earth,
In His eyes, each one of us, is equal in worth.

To receive His great blessings, we're asked to obey,
Which is not always easy, with things life throws your way.

There are times, when the people you know, let you down,
But God's true to His promises; there, great comfort is found.

We all make mistakes; but burdens don't have to last,
God forgives, if we seek Him; He puts our sins in the past.

When we're facing issues; whether they're big or they're small,
You can call on the Lord; He cares for them all.

And if things don't work out, the way we think they should,
Know that God works, all things, together for good.

People notice the difference, when God's Word's in your heart,
Finding joy, knowing Jesus, is what sets us apart.

---

*"But those who do what is right come to the light gladly,
so everyone can see they're doing what God wants." (NLT)
- John 3:21*

My Friend

When you meet certain people, you know instantly,
Your friendship is something, that's just meant to be.
With a foundation of mutual trust and respect,
Knowing what you see, is always, what you get.

A friend that can balance the give and the take,
And celebrate the achievements the other one makes.
The comfort of knowing, without a doubt,
They'd go to great lengths to help you out.

Through challenges and triumphs at work and at home;
The obstacles and changes, from which we have grown;
Through times of great sorrow and times of joy too,
Your prayers and support, have helped see me through.

You listen intently, you offer advice,
You're my shoulder to cry on, when words won't suffice.
Fond memories are built in the time that we spend,
What an honor it is, to call you my friend.

"...love your neighbor as yourself.
No other commandment is greater than these." (NLT)
- Mark 12:31

What God Joins Together

Fifty years of marriage, have come and gone,
It doesn't seem possible, that it's been this long!

This union, has bound you, through thick and through thin,
Through the lows of life's valleys and back up again.

As measured, by the world's standards today,
Staying with someone this long; it seems there's no way!

When the going gets tough, it's so easy to leave,
It's better than working things out (some believe.)

But there's more to a marriage (when God is your guide,)
It's not a commitment you can just set aside.

Two lives that are joined, together as one,
By God the Father, and His Holy Son.

No one (including a husband or wife),
Is to break up this union - God joins you for life.

The fruit of your marriage: the lives, together, you've changed,
The children who proudly carry on your good name,

Guests you've always made feel right at home,
The caring for family and friends you have shown.

Time has strengthened your love in a special way,
Your example proves marriage can still last today.

God's blessings are yours, and to your children they're passed,
When you keep your lives focused on making it last.

---

*"And may the LORD make your love grow
and overflow to each other and to everyone else,
just as our love overflows toward you." (NLT)*
- 1 Thessalonians 3:12

I Love The Lord

I Love the Lord, I Love the Lord, I Love the Lord God Almighty.
I Love the Lord, I Love the Lord, I Love the Lord God Almighty.

He's with me in trials; He's there by my side,
All things for His purpose; with His Spirit to guide.
His love it is faithful, His love never ends,
My Lord my Redeemer; He's my counselor my friend.

I Love the Lord, I Love the Lord, I Love the Lord God Almighty.
I Love the Lord, I Love the Lord, I Love the Lord God Almighty.

His son lived among us; in His perfect will,
And though sent to the cross, He's alive with us still.
Such peace knowing Jesus; Let's worship and sing,
Sing Glory to the Father; and all Praise to our King!

I Love the Lord, I Love the Lord, I Love the Lord God Almighty.
I Love the Lord, I Love the Lord, I Love the Lord God Almighty

---

"Shout joyful praises to God, all the earth!
Sing about the glory of his name!" (NLT)
- Psalm 66:1-2

Full Moon

"Those who are wise will shine as bright as the sky,
and those who turn many to righteousness will shine like stars forever."
(NLT)
- Daniel 12:3

Man On A Mission

The Bible tells of the great command,
Jesus' story is to be taken, to every land.

As Christians, we're all called to serve,
To share the truth, of God's Holy Word.

Around the corner, or around the world in Napal,
When God gives us the chance, do we answer His call?

Unsung heroes serve in places near (and some far),
Boldly sharing the Good News, wherever they are.

Not to their own desires, but to God's will they yield,
As they dedicate their lives, to the mission field.

Against warriors for Christ, the world puts up a fight,
Darkness isn't too pleased, when it's exposed by the light.

Beyond understanding, a special peace they know,
For God goes with them, wherever they go.

Such an inspiration, for others to see,
Through their sacrifice, God gets the glory.

Recognition; infrequent; despite their success,
But these ambassadors for Christ, are eternally blessed.

---

*"But when the Holy Spirit come upon you,
you will receive power and will tell people about me everywhere –
in Jerusalem, throughout Judea, in Samaria, into the ends of the earth." (NLT)
- Acts 1:8*

A Living Testimony

When the video, of your life, is played,
Will you be proud of all the decisions you've made?

In earth's contest for wealth, and the credit to claim,
Is time taken to pray, and to praise the Lord's name?

To stay in control, do you go to great lengths?
(Patience, for God's timing, is not one of our strengths.)

In the race to succeed, did you ever forget,
Time with loved ones, once lost, you will always regret.

What are you trying, so hard, to "achieve,"
When the gift most precious, is free for those who believe.

What's important in life, is not what we gain,
There is no place in Heaven for fortune or fame.

Your testimony of faith, through actions is "heard,"
Have you claimed God's promises; are you living His Word?

So that, when your final day is done,
God brings you home, your victory now won.

---

*"And you yourself must be an example to them by doing good deeds of every kind.
Let everything you do reflect the integrity and seriousness of your teaching." (NLT)*
- Titus 2:7

Where The Rubber Meets The Road

Thirty-six weeks out of fifty-two,
From track to track 'till the season's through.

It's easy for anyone to see,
Their love for the sport and the camaraderie.

The team is as close as family,
Sharing both the losses and the victories.

Men of courage; men of faith,
Ensure their car is both fast and safe.

Once the marshal starts the race,
Going breakneck speeds at a record pace.

A car spins out; the caution begins,
A decision to pit may determine who wins.

Split second choices made by the crew,
Could mean passing someone (or them passing you.)

Is the car too high; are the shocks too tight?
The crew chief has to get it right.

Just the slightest pressure change,
Could get them into Victory Lane.

Tires changed at record speeds,
So no one overtakes their lead.

With God-given instincts and driving skills,
Comes that awesome feeling; sweet victory's thrill!

Blessings shared generously with family and friends,
Which mean the most to them in the end.

They're a shining light for others to see,
As God gets the glory in all they achieve.

"And let us run with endurance the race that God has set before us.
We do this by keeping our eyes on Jesus,
on whom our faith depends from start to finish. (NLT)
- Hebrews 12:1b-2

Have I Made God Smile?

I pray each morning, as my day begins,
That my actions reflect God's spirit within.

Is quiet time first, as to how time's spent,
Am I a source of love and encouragement?

When I'm seeking answers, do I stop and pray?
Do I let God take control of all the things I say?

Do I delight in helping others (with no debt to repay),
Am I a faithful witness, to those I meet along the way?

With each chance given, do I reflect God's grace?
Is a sense of joy reflected, by the look on my face?

Is my measure of success, when the work is done,
Based on whether I've glorified God and His Son?

Does peace knowing Jesus, make my life worthwhile?
Looking back on my day, have I made God smile?

"Let heaven fill your thoughts.
Do not think only about things down here on earth."(NLT)
- Colossians 3:2

The Price Of Freedom

It seems so surreal; the war has begun,
We're counting on our native daughters and sons.
They're defending our freedom; ambassadors for peace,
Steadfast; on to victory; when, the fighting will cease.

One day, we're arguing about what they will wear,
Next, the fate of our nation, rests in their care.
Many, with high school, just barely complete,
Become brave men and women, who'll bring the enemy's defeat.

It's hard to believe, in our middle class world,
The kind of hatred and violence that evil's unfurled.
Though, as it is with war, some lives will be lost,
Those defending our freedom, know it's well worth the cost.

In our temporal world, the price of freedom is high,
But the rewards are eternal, when this life passes by.
Pray the lost find the Lord, through disciples of Christ,
So salvation's assured, for lives lost in this fight.

We have superior training, equipment; best in its class,
But it's our Leaders' focus on God, that brings victory at last.
The fervent prayers of our Nation, to God and His Son,
Will be the means by which the victory is won.

*"Remain faithful even when facing death,
and I will give you the crown of life." (NLT)
- Revelation 2:10*

From Whom All Blessings Flow

God is gracious; God is good,
He fulfills His promises, as He said He would.
God desires our trust; He wants our every travail,
So often, we only seek help, when our own efforts fail,

There are times God answers our prayers with a NO,
He calls us to follow, where He asks us to go.
God may lead us places, where our outcome's unsure,
But if he asks us to go, He will help us endure.

At times it's a struggle, just to get through the day.
We pray that God will take all our suffering away.
If God made our life easy, and every contest we'd win,
It would be harder to see, all things good come from Him.

God has orchestrated events in my life recently,
So I could witness to others, how He's working in me.
Let me not take for granted, God's mercy and grace,
Keep my thanks for this blessing always in the right place.

God is at work all around us; looking back we will see,
It's through trials, He helps us live more faithfully.
I praise God for each moment of life that He gives,
Each one molding my heart, into one more like His.

---

*"For God is working in you, giving you the desire to obey him
and the power to do what pleases him." (NLT)*
- Philippians 2:13

Walking The Word

We're taught to be, a guiding light,
A reflection of Jesus; to do what is right.

And though we have learned, the way we should act,
Temptation grows stronger, when we're under attack.

It takes courage, and beliefs that are strong,
To turn away from doing, things you know that are wrong.

Confidently walking, with God's Word as your shield,
No matter what taking a stand might yield.

In a world that says, "following the crowd is best,"
He, who walks by God's word, is blessed.

"Show me the path I should walk, O LORD.
Point out the right road to follow." (NLT)
- Psalm 25:4

I Pray Each Day

I pray each day, to thank you; for all you've done for me,
The gift of life; the morning light; for friends and family.
I pray daily for this country and the leaders of our land,
For healing and for wisdom, from your almighty hand.

I pray for those who've done me wrong or caused me any pain,
Help me forgive; reveal your love, so next time, they'll refrain.
I pray each day for others; their needs as great as mine,
For encouragement and comfort in the most difficult of times.

I pray each day, for strength I need to help me make it through,
To let go of things done my way and give up control to you.
I pray each day, you search my heart for un-repented sin,
So there's a pure and holy place for you to dwell within.

I pray, that I can find the blessings, when life seems too hard to live,
For peace, beyond all human power, that only you can give.
I pray each day, it's not my will, but yours that will be done,
That I take time to stop and listen, to you, Most Holy One.

I pray each day, I read your Word; that on my heart, it will be sealed,
So my life reflects your glory; your love, and grace, revealed,
I pray each day, I trust you and walk your path of truth and light,
For you to guide me daily to help me live as Christ.

"Keep alert and pray.
Otherwise temptation will overpower you.
For though the spirit is willing enough, the body is weak!" (NLT)
- Matthew 26:41

Of Faith And Freedom

Our nation "under God" has been blessed most graciously,
Though we often take for granted that we're a people living free.
Soldiers have been defending freedom throughout our history,
To preserve our right to prosper in this "Land of Liberty."

For the cause of freedom; we send our soldiers out to fight
Obediently following the path God's laid, by faith and not by sight.
They fight, not because they have to, but because "In God they trust,"
They courageously fight for freedom for every one of us.

They've faced some situations; insurmountable at best,
Which challenged them, to keep the faith, in the midst of such a test.
Courage; elusive on their own, but in Him they can do all things,
He gives the faithful strength to face whatever this life brings.

With God given courage, our country's freedom they defend,
No greater love hath any man than to lay his life down for a friend.
Soldiers' lives have been the price by which our freedom has been paid,
Heavenly treasures await these heroes for sacrifices that they've made.

Overtime, the scars of battle begin to take their toll,
But peace comes with wisdom, knowing, that our God is in control.
God calls us to bow, in fervent prayer, for the healing of our land,
He promises to restore it, when we acknowledge His command.

Some people feel that churches should be separate from "the states,"
But it's a heritage of Christianity that makes our country great.
Forefathers used the Word of God as a firm foundation for this land,
The doctrines which were drafted then are still the ones on which we stand.

Jesus obediently surrendered, His life for you and me,
His death upon the cross cleansed us from all iniquities.
His sacrifice was the only way He could set His people free,
So believers could commune with God throughout eternity.

Our country's courageous heroes, through their own sacrifice,
Give us just a glimpse of what it means, to live your life as Christ.
Rewarded for their faith, these soldiers never walked alone,
A place of honor's waiting for them when they reach their Heavenly home.

"So there is a special rest still waiting for the people of God." (NLT)
- Hebrews 4:9

Acknowledgements

It is so hard to single out those of you who went the extra mile to encourage me to continue writing and to pursue publishing my poems... because SO MANY OF YOU HAVE! I would be remiss, however, if I didn't especially thank my dearest "Angel" and teacher Bettie Holley (who has more wisdom in her little finger than I have accumulated in my 46 years; but who makes you feel absolutely at peace in her presence.) Oh, the things I have learned from that sweet and special soul (and her handsome Marine and most righteous husband Henry.)

As a member of the body of Christ at Johnson Ferry Baptist Church in Marietta, GA, I have been graciously blessed by the steadfast dedication to Christ-centered preaching and teaching. The tremendous focus on prayer as the power source for our ministries staff and our members is a rich part of the heritage of this church. I am constantly in awe of how God works so powerfully through the prayer warriors on the church prayer team as well as through the precious prayers and support of many special "Angels" in my Sunday school class (and many of their spouses) and teachers and friends from many terrific weekday Bible study classes and networking groups. Thank you for helping with every aspect of this project (including finding helpers, typing and formatting the poems, proofreading, and the list goes on.)

I want to express sincere appreciation to my awesome circle of friends and sweet sisters in Christ: Ann, Jody, Lynn, Su, Betsy and Joy for being great sounding boards and resources of wisdom to keep me on track. Thanks to so many other family members, friends and business associates who have offered their encouragement, support and prayers for me to take the leap of faith to share my poetry in a book. And a special thank you to Ted Sprague for his direction in developing a theme for my poetry book. Through your vision for my poetry, this book is now becoming a reality.

A note of thanks absolutely must go out to Mr. Decker Anstrom, COO, Landmark Communications, Inc. (parent company of The Weather Channel.) Decker has been an incredible mentor (helping me grow my skills as an emerging leader in the industry and helping me keep my values and priorities in perspective to achieve a work/life balance), a patient teacher (not only about the industry but also teaching me "the ropes" for political advocates - lobbying in DC, etc.), an authentic role model (he is one of the few people I know who actually lives what he "preaches") and a valued friend; always quick to send his "trademark" handwritten notes from his heart; making sure to thank you for each contribution made to the company, to acknowledge personal milestones and to offer his personal support in my fight against Parkinson's (both he and his wonderful wife Sherry have attended numerous fundraisers including the Mo Udall Awards Dinner and the Parkinson's Unity Walk.)

And finally, a special acknowledgement of my dear friend and mentor, Lynn Price... for sharing her contacts at Inkwater Press and her inspiration (just Lynn being Lynn!). I hope you know what an impact you have made on my life and on the lives of those with whom you share yourself so generously at Camp to Belong...and amazingly, never at the expense of the focus and time that you devote to your own children & family. Thanks for lighting a fire under me and showing me by your example, what a blessing this project would be.

With my love and deepest appreciation,
Tamra Cantore

"It is not that we think we can do anything of lasting value by ourselves.
Our only power and success come from God." (NLT)
- 2 Corinthians 3:5

Appendix

CHAPTER ONE
STORM SHELTER

The Sacrificial Lamb   February 3, 2004
>   Written for the inaugural "Glimpses of Glory" gallery display at our church. The theme for the display was "He was the ransom for many." We were challenged to use our God-given gifts to make visible, an invisible God.

Where Jesus Dwells   September 9, 2001
>   Written as a gift for Bettie and Henry's house-warming party following a major remodeling of their home.

Through Jesus Alone   January 5, 2001
>   Written following a New Year's Day Sermon.

Fear Not   April 4, 2002
>   Flying for the first time after September 11; my husband questioned why a person of faith would be afraid.

We're Not Alone   April 12, 2003
>   A friend, Cheryl, asked if I had a poem she could give one of her acquaintances to comfort her as she was dealing with the loss of a child. I didn't already have one but God laid this poem on my heart.

One Prayer Away   January 28, 2000
>   Written following Bettie's Sunday School lesson which challenged us to be confident in our salvation.

Jesus   October 16, 2001
>   Written following a Sunday School discussion about who Jesus was.

Chapter Two
Warnings and Advisories

A Prayer for the New Millennium   December 30, 1999
> Written during a time of reflection as the new millennium was approaching.

If You Knew What You Were Missing   January 26, 2004
> A time of reflection about close friends and family members who were not living the abundant life promised by Christ when we turn our lives and our trust to the Lord.

Just a Fleeting Moment   June 10, 2000
> A close friend and co-worker, Wendy, lost her fight with Breast Cancer. Her family asked for this poem to be read at her funeral.

Mommy   August 5, 2001
> A time of reflection on my children's behavior and my role as their Mother.

It's About Time   February 6, 2004
> A time of reflection about how hectic life has become and how that is affecting our relationships.

Words   May 23, 3004
> Written following a discussion about the power of the tongue from our Sunday School study of the book of James.

Today's Prayer   March 14, 2000
> Written during a time of reflection about my children's walk with the Lord. I wanted to encourage them to count their blessings and pray with expectation for God to fulfill his promises.

Have We Made a Difference?   July 5, 2000
> Written following the first advocacy event that I had attended in Washington, DC for the Parkinson's Action Network.

Search My Heart   June 24, 2004

Written from notes found during the publishing process for this book from a time of reflection about how I spent my time.

Without Christ   September 15, 2003

Written following one of Bettie's lessons in Sunday School.

Am I Thankful?   November 23, 2000

As a part of a Family Tradition, we asked each person that was visiting for Thanksgiving to write down what they were Thankful for. These were my comments.

The Perfect Gift   December 7, 2000

A time of reflection after Bryant Wright's sermon on the true meaning of Christmas.

CHAPTER THREE
RAINY DAYS

Take it to the Lord   January 10, 2003

Written for a family member who was struggling with a decision.

Letting Go   May 15, 2000

A time in my life when I wanted to follow God's will but just didn't want to let go of control of my life.

Can we see God?   July 12, 2002

A time of reflection about slowing down and looking for the ways God is working all around us.

"My" Will be Done   July 22, 2001

Written for a Christian friend who was facing a major life decision.

Lord, Why Me?   September 4, 2000

At a time when I just couldn't understand why God had allowed some of the trials in my life.

He Cares for You With Love   February 9, 2000
    Written for my half brother, James, who was in the hospital.

Quiet Moments   April 15, 2001
    Written at a time of reflection about the hectic family routine.

Forget You Not   December 2, 2002
    Written at a time when I no longer could do all the things that I
    wanted to do because of my deteriorating condition.

He Dries Our Tears   January 28, 2000
    Written for my Mother as she was waiting on some test results.

CHAPTER FOUR
RAINBOWS

At Times Like This   October 29, 2002
    Written for a dear friend, Donna, who had lost her father. Though I
    never met her father, God gave me words that reflected her father's
    faithful Christian walk and the love he had for his family.

Blessings Fell Like Rain   April 28, 2003
    Written as I was reflecting on my experience at the 3rd Parkinson's
    Unity Walk in which TEAM CANTORE participated.

I'm on my Way to Heaven   November 12, 2000
    I never met the gentleman for whom I wrote this poem, however, I
    know his sweet wife, Jane, and God kept telling me it was some-
    thing I should do. Before Gene died, he and my friend shared the
    words God had spoken to me. This poem (which I often refer to as
    "Gene's Poem") has been such a blessing to so many people who
    have lost their loved ones.

Lady Liberty   September 13, 2001
    On the day after September 11, God gave me these words to help me
    sort through what had happened.

What's a Girl To Do   December 5, 2002
This was written for my Mother as she was agonizing over her retirement.

Rising Above   February 14, 2000
This poem was written originally to my husband for Valentine's Day but I have also used it many times as a wedding gift.

The Blessing of my Burden   February 25, 2001
This was written as a result of an overwhelming sense of humble appreciation for everyone who supported TEAM CANTORE the first year we participated in the Parkinson's Unity Walk.

When Angels Pray   April 22, 2001
This was written when I was pondering the responsibilities of being asked to be the prayer leader for my Sunday School class.

CHAPTER FIVE
SNOWFLAKES

God's Masterpiece   July 7, 2002
Written after a lesson about how God sees us from the Group Study "Discovery: God's answers to your deepest questions" by Will Wyatt.

Not One More Minute   August 11, 2000
Written to my Father after Brian (a work associate) had shared the story of losing his Dad with me in an emotional conversation at work one day.

Grandma   April 4, 2001
Written about my late maternal Grandmother to honor her and as a gift to my Grandfather on his 95th Birthday.

Someday, Grandpa   April 4, 2001
Written as a gift for my Grandfather's 95th Birthday. This poem was read at his memorial service .

Elizabeth   August 10, 2000
   Written for my niece who lived with us a couple of summers to help out with the kids.

Christina - Ballerina   May 5, 2002
   Written for my daughter on the occasion of her dance recital.

Henry   September 13, 2002
   Written to honor my friend, Henry, on his Birthday.

Bettie   November 22, 2003
   My Sunday School class asked me to write this poem to honor my sweet angel and teacher on her Birthday. She is the epitome of the fruits of the Spirit. What an honor and a blessing it was for me to write this for her.

There's Always Hope   June 13, 2002
   Written in memory of a dear work associate and role model, John Hope, to give his family at his memorial service.

More Than Meets the Eye   April 26, 2004
   Written for actor Michael J. Fox with the utmost respect for his unselfish efforts to fund research to find a cure for this horrible degenerative condition we are mutually fighting. What a sincere and caring gentleman he has proven to be.

CHAPTER SIX
SUNNY SKIES

For the Beauty of the Earth   July 4, 2003
   Written early one morning as I was vacationing with my family and some dear friends in the mountains one 4th of July weekend. This poem was part of the second "Glimpses of Glory" exhibit at our church under the theme of "God in Nature."

Friendship's Blessing   November 11, 2000
   Written for my two "sisters" (Ann and Jody) who may not be blood relatives but have been my family here in Georgia for as long as I've known them. They have been the two who have been holding up my arms to give me the ability to continue to stand.

God's Miracle of Birth February 11, 2000
> Written for Mary (a dear co-worker and friend) on the occasion of her baby shower when she was expecting her first child.

Heaven Sent an Angel November 11, 2000
> This was written as a gift to special co-workers and friends (Joyclyn, Linda, Lorraine and Mary) for all they had done for me.

Steamboat July 20, 2003
> Written following a family vacation at Steamboat which left such wonderful memories.

Joyful in Jesus August 10, 2000
> Written after a Sunday School lesson regarding the peace and joy found living as Christ.

My Friend March 16, 2001
> Written on the occasion of a going away party for Bob (one of my best friends and mentors at work.)

What God Joins Together November 16, 2001
> Written for my in-laws 50th Wedding Anniversary Celebration.

I Love the Lord June 10, 2000
> I literally was woken up in the middle of the night by angles singing these words in my ears.

CHAPTER SEVEN
FULL MOON

Man on a Mission May 25, 2002
> Written for some incredible missionaries, Bruce and Micki, whom our Sunday School class supports.

A Living Testimony September 4, 2000
> Written as I was reflecting upon how I had been living my life.

Where the Rubber Meets the Road November 21, 2000
> Written out of respect for my friend, 2000 NASCAR Nextel Cup Champion, Bobby Labonte.

Have I made God Smile?   February 14, 2001
> Written after my daughter asked me after her prayers if she had made God Smile.

The Price of Freedom   March 20, 2003
> Written at the time we entered the Iraqi War. This poem was dedicated to my step-brother Mac's son, Ryan, my niece Beth's husband, Marcus and to my friend Cary's son J.P.

From Whom All Blessings Flow   August 22, 2003
> Written as praise for some incredible things God was doing in my life.

Walking the Word   February 22, 2000
> Written for my half-brother, Richie, who was being ridiculed by his hockey team for his Christian values, but refused to back down or go with the crowd.

I Pray Each Day   August 20, 2002
> Written during a Bible Study by Beth Moore "Beloved Disciple."

Of Faith and Freedom   April 14, 2004
> Written at the request of Brian Hedrick, Minister of Instrumental Music at my church to be read during an arrangement of the same name as a way of introducing our guest speaker, Clebe McClary, during our church's American Celebration service for 4th of July.

Resources

Facts About Parkinson's Disease

Parkinson's disease (PD) is a progressive neurological disorder. In PD the cells that produce the neuro-chemical dopamine degenerate, causing tremor, muscle stiffness or rigidity, slowness of movement (brady-kinesia) and loss of balance.

Although medication masks some symptoms for a limited period, generally 4 to 8 years, they begin causing side effects. Eventually, the medications lose their effectiveness, leaving the victim unable to move, speak or swallow.

More than one million Americans are affected with this disease—approximately 40% under the age of 60 years old.

There are 60,000 cases diagnosed each year—one every 9 minutes.

People used to think of PD as an older person's disease—people like Michael J. Fox are living proof that PD can occur at any age.

Celebrities who have PD include: Michael J. Fox, Janet Reno, the Pope, Billy Graham and Muhammad Ali.

Although the cause of Parkinson's is unclear, a combination of genetic and environmental factors may be involved. Currently, there is no cure—but there is great hope for the future. Researchers have made significant advances. Currently there are clinical trials going on in gene therapy; neural growth factors and surgical therapies such as Deep Brain Stimulation (DBS) There are also several new drugs in the pipeline.

Ten years ago the National Institutes of Health were spending less than $25 per patient per year on Parkinson's research—TODAY, NIH spends close to $250 per patient per year on research. It is not enough, but we are making progress.

In late 2002, The National Institute of Environmental Health Services (NIEHS) granted $20 million in grants to three research centers to study the relationship between exposure to environmental agents and the development of PD.

(Information courtesy of the Parkinson's Unity Walk)

Facts About Team Cantore and The Parkinson's Unity Walk

The purpose of the Parkinson's Unity Walk is to raise money for Parkinson's research. Since its inception, corporate sponsors have paid for the walk's expenses allowing the Parkinson's Unity Walk organizers the ability to give 100% of all donations directly to research. This is a tradition that they are proud to say has continued to be maintained, which sets them apart from many other charity organizations. By visiting the Parkinson's Unity Walk website at www.unitywalk.org you can review where the research dollars are being use and on which research projects. There are 7 major Parkinson organizations that receive funds from the Walk:

1. American Parkinson Disease Association (APDA) www.apdaparkinson.org
2. National Parkinson Foundation (NPF) www.parkinson.org
3. Parkinson's Action Network (PAN) www.parkinsonaction.org
4. The Michael J. Fox Foundation for Parkinson's Research www.michaeljfox.org
5. The Parkinson Alliance www.parkinsonalliance.net
6. The Parkinson's Institute www.thepi.org
7. Parkinson's Disease Foundation www.pdf.org

Tamra Cantore is the Founder and Team Captain of TEAM CANTORE (a fund-raising team for Parkinson's research) which has participated in the Parkinson's Unity Walk for the past four years. Since its formation, TEAM CANTORE has raised more than $100,000 for Parkinson's Research and has secured over $1M of in-kind cable advertising from key cable Affiliates to promote the Parkinson's Unity Walk in NYC. TEAM CANTORE has enlisted the support of The Weather Channel® to increase the exposure for the event and to educate the public as to the promise of Parkinson's research and critical need for funding. The Weather Channel has provided resources to produce Public Service

Announcements (PSAs) to promote the event, has done a segments which have aired on The Weather Channel regarding the environmental toxicity research being done related to Parkinson's and has provided live on-site coverage of this event to past two years. Tamra's husband, meteorologist, Jim Cantore, has served as The Weather Channel spokesperson for Parkinson's related activity. He will be joined by ESPN Commentator, Stuart Scott, in PSA's promoting the 2005 Unity Walk. Donations are collected year-round. You can go to the Unity Walk website at www.unitywalk.org to search for and sponsor a walker or to join a team so you can participate in the next Parkinson's Unity Walk. (Remember, 100% of all donations made to sponsor walkers go directly toward Parkinson's research.)

TEAM CANTORE also commissioned a Parkinson's Unity Walk Logo Keepsake (charm, pendant and lapel pin) which can be ordered off of the www.unitywalk.org web site. This project was completely underwritten by CIGNA HEALTHCARE so that 100% of every dollar paid for the Keepsake can go directly to Parkinson's research.

Facts About Fragile X Syndrome

Fragile X Syndrome is the most common form of inherited mental retardation. Over 1 million people are affected worldwide - roughly 1 in 4,000 males and 1 in 8,000 females. One in 400 females carries the mutated gene that can cause Fragile X - roughly 8 million carriers. The impact upon individuals and families is huge.

While millions of people are affected by Fragile X, it is an obscure disorder because there are no pronounced physical attributes. Men are affected more severely due to having only one X chromosome. Symptoms range from mild learning disabilities (such as attention deficit disorder) to severe retardation. Symptoms may also include behavioral problems, connective tissue disorders, extreme shyness and avoidance of eye contact/squinting.

Research funding is critical to further understand Fragile X and to develop a therapeutic cure. With this in mind, Rick Reynolds established the Reynolds Fragile X Research Fund at the Emory University School of Medicine in Atlanta. Its goal is to help fund the groundbreaking research led by Stephen Warren, Ph.D. Emory University is the world leader in Fragile X research. Emory's strengths include:

1) The discovery of the Fragile X gene (by Dr. Stephen Warren in 1991),
2) More researchers dedicated to Fragile X research than anywhere else in the world and
3) The recipient of the only National Institutes of Health (NIH) program project on Fragile X. This means that funding has been released to oversee multiple studies.

Research institutions like Emory have achieved remarkable results with limited resources. It has opened doors to cutting edge solutions. Breakthroughs are on the horizon that will dramatically improve, and perhaps eliminate, the devastating effects of Fragile X upon individuals and families. Additional funding will significantly propel efforts to achieve therapeutic solutions and treatments.

The research fund is managed by Emory University. Tax deductible contributions may be sent to:

The Reynolds Fragile X Research Fund
Emory University School of Medicine
Attention: Natalie Walker
1440 Clifton Road, NE; Suite 116
Atlanta, GA 30322

Checks are to be made payable to Emory University with "The Reynolds Fragile X Research Fund, # 6-33717" in the memo line.

Facts About Right from the Heart

Right From The Heart is a non-denominational, non profit corporation formed for the expressed purpose of reaching and discipling people for Jesus Christ. This mission is being accomplished using radio, television, print media and the internet.

Right From The Heart Ministries literally began, in 1992 in the heart of Bryant Wright, Senior Pastor of the 6,500 member Johnson Ferry Baptist Church. With a few networking contacts, the ministry commenced broadcasting the half-hour teaching program on Christian radio in Atlanta. Later that year, the first one-minute spot aired on secular radio.

Today, Right From The Heart continues its mission of reaching and discipling people for Jesus Christ by utilizing radio, television, print media and the Internet..

"Reaching" to the secular market is done through quick hitting one-minute inspirational radio and television spots. These inspirational short messages are played in metro Atlanta and heard throughout Georgia on the 115 stations of the Georgia News Network. Additionally, the one-minute spots are heard on adult contemporary and Top 40 stations in 67 cities each Sunday morning on the national syndicated show "Sonrise."

"Reaching" is also done with 30-second and one-minute television spots which run an average of 50 times each month metro Atlanta television and selected cable channels. A daily devotional along with the television spots are available for online viewing seven days a week at www.rfth.org. There is even an option of sending these links to a friend.

"Discipling" is accomplished by providing sound Biblical teaching to Christians. These half-hour radio programs highlight the 20-year pulpit ministry of Bryant Wright and are heard on Christian radio throughout metro Atlanta, Birmingham, Alabama and the Baltimore/Washington, D.C area. Sermon schedules are available online for both the radio listener and members of Johnson Ferry Baptist Church.

The strategy of Right From The Heart has been to establish and saturate the Atlanta market and then expand our growth on this proven model. The uniqueness of this ministry has successfully engaged our results-oriented and time restricted society by providing answers and insights to important contemporary issues.

Today, Right From The Heart messages are played in the USA as well as in Asia and Africa.

Right From The Heart is a member of the National Religious Broadcasters (NRB) and the Evangelical Council for Financial Accountability (ECFA).

(Information courtesy of Right from the Heart - www.rfth.org)

The Plan of Salvation

From the time of the original sin in the Garden of Eden, man has been born to this world as a sinner.

No matter how hard we try, we can't "buy" our salvation by anything of our own doing.

Without a relationship with Jesus Christ, we are destined to spend eternity apart from God.

The good news of Jesus Christ is that God sent him to die in our place so that we could be free from our sins.

> *"For God so loved the world that he gave his only Son so that everyone who believes in him will not perish but have eternal life."(NLT)*
>
> *- John 3:16*

If we are willing to admit our need for Jesus to cleanse us from our sins, and

If we believe that Jesus was the Savior who died for us on the cross, then rose from the grave

> *"Jesus told him, "I am the way, the truth, and the life. No one can come to the Father except through me."(NLT)*
>
> *- John 14:6*

we can ask God for forgiveness of our sins with a heart of repentance (or a desire to turn from our sins)

and, In God 's grace, by our faith, He promises us eternal life with Him in Heaven.

> *"For the wages of sin is death, but the free gift of God is eternal life through Christ Jesus our Lord."(NLT)*
>
> *- Romans 6:23*

We believe that we are all saved the same way, by the special favor
of the Lord Jesus." (NLT)
- Acts 15:11

Once you pray to accept Jesus into your heart, He will control your
life through the Holy Spirit."

"But I will send you the Counselor – the Spirit of truth. He will come
to you from the Father and will tell you all about me."(NLT)
-John 15:26

Be sure and share your decision with your pastor or a Christian
friend so they can help you find a Bible teaching church or class for
you to learn more about growing in your faith and in your relation-
ship with Jesus.